WA

TOWARDS

FINANCIAL FREEDOM

Romona M. Hale-Coley, MBA

ISBN 978-0-692-43381-2

Scottrade Trading Brokerage Account

Earn three (3) **FREE** online trades when you open a Scottrade account using code ICRO7847. Log on to www.scottrade.com to redeem. Even better, once you refer a family member, friend or coworker who opens an account, you'll receive three more free trades. Scottrade, Inc., is a member of FINRA/SIPC and FDIC. Romona Hale-Coley (Team Coley Designs LLC) and Scottrade are separate and not affiliated.

For supplemental data and additional examples:

*Log onto **www.walkingtowardsfinancialfreedom.com***

*Follow me on Instagram **@iam_romona***

*Follow me on Twitter **@rhalecoley***

*Like me on Facebook @ **Walking Towards Financial Freedom***

This book is dedicated to my mother, Elizabeth Hale, who inspired me to reach for greatness and be the best person I can be. First and foremost, she taught me to be a good human being, to be kind, to love. Second, to never be afraid to ask for what it is that I desired because the worst that someone can say is, "No." Lastly, to always be willing to help someone less fortunate than we are. For these life lessons, I am truly blessed and forever grateful.

In loving memory of my father, Ramon Antonio Gonzalez, you're always close to my heart.

PREFACE

I've always had a passion for the world of finance. Growing up in the inner city of north Philadelphia gave me an unwavering determination to achieve a career in Corporate Finance. It was during an economics class, at Dobbins Randolph Vocational High school, when I experienced a pivotal and defining moment which created a spark in me. I had a teacher named Mr. Herter who was filling in for the permanent teacher that was out sick. During his coverage of my economics class he brought a copy of the Wall Street Journal into class and introduced it to us. He gave us a brief overview on the format of treasury, municipal, mortgage and corporate bonds. The beauty of this moment, for me, was that the teacher was a white male in a classroom of all African Americans children. This was not a topic outlined on the syllabus or lesson plan. He knew he would get resistance from students who would not be interested in learning, which he did, but I can recall so clearly his advice to those students. He held the paper up and said, "We're going to read the investment section and learn how treasury securities are listed and quoted in the Wall Street Journal. For those of you who are not interested, you can put your heads down. But please don't prevent those who are interested from learning." I recall there were some students who did put their heads down. For me, it was like waiting for a treasured prize. I knew what this type of exposure meant. It meant that I could learn just as much as someone with an elite education from different ends of the world. Not only could I learn it, but I could be great at it. It could be my saving grace. There would be no excuse for me not to succeed.

When you're a child, the influence of a positive adult is priceless. I'm sure he had no idea of the life changing moment that one day of class had on me. During my senior year in high school, I would also have the opportunity to work as an intern after school for Betty Smith, an entrepreneur and financial planner. The spark that was created by my economics teacher was further fueled by my new mentor, who I would learn an invaluable deal from.

Fast forward a decade or so later. I am a graduate from Pennsylvania State University with a Bachelor's degree in Finance and International Business. A few weeks before graduation, I was offered a position with a publicly traded corporation in their Finance Management Trainee program. I have held several accounting roles and went on to pursue and complete my MBA and ultimately transition as a Senior Financial Analyst in Corporate Treasury for a global company.

I am now stay-at-home mom to a baby girl with the most important job of all thus far. I have been blessed to come full circle in my life. It is now my calling to share the experiences that I've had in the corporate finance and accounting and teach others how I took key concepts learned and utilized them to managing my personal finances. I truly feel that it's my obligation and mission to share this information with my community, especially women. But also to anyone who is interested in the journey to financial freedom. My hope is that this book will reach people across the world to inspire, empower and change lives.

CONTENTS

<u>BONUS CHAPTERS:</u>

Chapter I...SAVERS VERSUS SPENDERS

When addressing financial planning, there are generally two categories that individuals fall into. You're either a spender or a saver. Let's begin by defining the latter. Savers will deposit the majority of their income, after deducting monthly expenses, into a personal savings or checking's account. If you've identified yourself as a saver, the good news is that you're on the right track because you have developed the mindset of building financial security. The key now is to maximize the return of your savings by diversifying into several investment vehicles, which have remarkably higher returns than a personal savings account. The goal is to have several income streams with positive cash flow. In other words, you want your money to work for you.

Maybe you're on the opposite end of the spectrum and have a tendency to spend more than you save. Let's generalize spenders. If you are a spender, you may find yourself making frequent unnecessary impulse purchases, and, most often, your expenses exceeds your income. As a result of poor spending habits, unfortunately, you may be living paycheck to paycheck. In either case, the key to financial freedom begins with an honest assessment of where you are with your personal finances. Once we identify ourselves as either a spender or a saver, we can then begin to examine our finances and implement smart "lifestyle" choices.

The reason I have chosen to use the term "lifestyle" instead of "financial" choices is because ultimately, financial choices becomes lifestyle choices when practiced consistently. Most people who are in debt are not necessarily in need of additional income, they are in need of making smarter financial decisions, on a daily basis. This then transitions into habit and transcends into lifestyle choices. For example, let's consider spending $10 per day on lunch five days a week. When we look at $10 in isolation by itself, it seems measly. Most of us would not consider $10 to be a large quantity of money or extreme spending. However, when we consider the impact of this spending habit on an annual basis, the same $10 equates to $2,600 per year. If you married, this then doubles to $5,200 per household if both of you practice this spending habit. Furthermore, if you're a married couple with school-aged children who receive a daily lunch allowance of just $5 per day, this increase the total household lunch expense by an additional $1,300 per child. Now you're spending a minimum of $6,500 per year just eating out for lunch. This can become a significant expense for middle income families, and certainly for low income households. When you annualize expenses and calculate them on a yearly basis, you can grasp the magnitude of a typical expense that most of us incur without giving it second thought.

We can implement simple, daily, lifestyle choices, such as taking lunch a few days a week, and invest the savings into an investment account, allowing us to earn money instead of spending it. On the other hand, poor choices can, and often, escalate to a mountain of debt in the long run. It's critical to implement smart lifestyle habits sooner than later. As the great poet Maya Angelou once said, "When you know better, you do better!"

The key to successfully maneuvering life's financial roadmap is to identify where you are and where you want to be. Next, consider what actions you need to implement to reach your financial goals. If your goal is to reach financial independence, we're on the journey together. I will share what I've learned in the following chapters.

Chapter II...FINANCIAL HEALTH

Most often when we hear the word "health," we instantly think of our physical well-being. It may be over whelming for some of us and not so much for others. Some of us may be in the middle of the road, while others are downright obsessed with their physique. We may count the number of calories we intake, determine if an item is low in carbs and sugars, examine food labels, further research to see if certain foods are gluten free or not. I can elaborate, but I'm sure I've painted a picture of one taking extreme measures to gain nutritional value from their diet. We can examine our financial health in a similar manner. We have to commit the same level of diligence to our financial well-being. Are we examining our fixed and variable expenses on a frequent basis? Are we reducing expenses and increasing savings and interest income for later years? We must equally dedicate time and energy to our financial health as well as our physical health. When we are proactive with our finances instead of reactive, it reduces the stress that impacts our physical health.

The simplest way to find out where we are in our financial assessment is to think of it as being a financial check-up. Let's begin with the simple questions:
Do you have at least 6 months to a year of living expenses for unforeseen emergencies?
- ✓ How prepared are you to cover expenses if you were to lose a job?
- ✓ Are my savings easily assessable and highly liquid?

4

In a nutshell, how prepared are you to handle both planned and unforeseen expenses? To answer these questions most accurately we need to compare our income to our expenses. Begin by listing all your monthly fixed expenses such as rent or mortgage, daycare, car notes, auto insurance, educational loans, etc. These expenses will remain the same, month over month. Next, list your monthly variable expenses, which fluctuate from month to month. Typically, your monthly utilities will fall into the variable expenses category. For example, for the month of January your heating bill may have been $150, but may go down to $120 the following month as it warms. Last, list all your discretionary monthly expenses such as entertainment, extracurricular activities, gym fees, personal upkeep such as hair, nails, waxing, etc. Before calculating your total expenses, notate your monthly income on the same sheet. I would suggest using a Microsoft Excel spreadsheet to make this simple to calculate and maintain a log to update month over month to track your progress.

This first step will speak volumes for where your financial journey begins. Once you've listed and totaled your monthly income and expenses, you'll have your first snapshot of your financial health. Now we can answer the key question:

✓ Do your expenses exceed your income?

For some of us the answer to the question is "No." This is obviously the ideal scenario that we all hope to be in. The reality is that many of us will answer "Yes" to that same question and will be shocked to see the disparity, or gap, by which our expenses exceed our income. What can we do to change this outcome?

I am going to introduce a few key financial ratios to help manage our personal finances. Most corporations use financial ratios to both assess and manage the financial strength and performance of their company. Individuals can also adopt some of these practices to assist with better understanding one's personal finances. I'll focus on liquidity and debt ratios. Don't be intimidated. We are going to use these tools to paint a picture of our financial health.

Before introducing these financial ratios, I will explain a few key terms. The first term is liquidity. *Liquidity* refers to how quickly an asset can be turned into cash. The next term is *assets*, which are anything of economic value that can be converted to cash. Cash is the most liquid asset. In personal finance, *current assets* can be readily or quickly turned into cash to pay any debt that is due within a short period of time, which is referred to as current liabilities. The last term we'll discuss is *current or short-term liability*, which is debt due within the year or sooner.

Now that we have those terms covered we'll move forward with understanding a few ratios. The first ratio we'll look at is *working capital* which is calculated by taking total current assets minus total current liabilities. It's one of the simplistic formulas that both individuals and corporations can use. Working Capital allows us to determine if one can meet and cover expenses due in the short-term. Next is *debt to asset* ratio which allows us to determine the amount of debt used to finance our assets. It is determined by taking

6

total liabilities divided by total assets. Generally speaking, a ratio under 1 means the majority of assets was acquired with cash rather than debt. A ratio greater than 1 means the majority of assets were financed mainly with debt. Individuals with high ratios have greater financial risk and creditors may not be willing to extend additional credit or loans. The last ratio I'll discuss is the current ratio. This is very important in determining how well we can meet short-term liabilities in the event of a financial emergency. **Current ratio** is equal to cash or cash equivalents divided by short-term liabilities. Let's illustrate using a simple example. You have current assets of $10,000 and current liabilities of $7,500. The current ratio is 1.33 which simply means our current assets are 1.33 times the value of our current liabilities. This is a fair position to be in but tells us we have used some debt to finance our assets.

Many of us may feel hesitant or overwhelmed to address the reality of our financial health head on. However, the truth is freeing. It allows us to take corrective actions and turn things around for the better. Once we see the picture we're painted, we can be the artist of our financial future and modify it. It's never too late to get it right. Living in financial turmoil is destructive, walking towards financial freedom may be long and winding, but the journey is gratifying and creates a feeling of empowerment!

Chapter III...HOW TO EFFECTIVELY USE CREDIT CARDS

This is probably one of the more exciting chapters for me to address because there is much debate and controversy surrounding whether the use of credit cards are good or bad. The issue of owning a credit card may not be a major one for most of us but, surprisingly, many minorities, in particular, do not own a major credit card. For those of us who do, we may only use it for emergency purposes. For others, we may rely on credit cards to purchase things we cannot afford. The fact is, many of us may have misused credit cards previously and, consequently, may have amassed massive debt.

Here's a *rule of thumb*, "If you do not have the cash to pay for the purchase you are going to put on your credit card, more than likely, you cannot afford it." This rule of thumb will help to reduce impulse buying and avoid unnecessary spending. As I've done continuously throughout the book, I'm going to ask you to be honest with yourself and apply the key points that are applicable to you.

When used correctly, there are numerous advantages in opting to use your credit card instead of cash. Many credit cards have cashback bonus rewards, travel incentives, gas purchase rewards, fraud coverage and no annual fees. Here are ways to optimize these advantages:

✓ *Pay Recurring Monthly Expenses*

You can set up payments online using your credit card for monthly expenses incurred such as utilities, mortgage, internet, etc. These are bills that have to be paid regardless of payment type.

Here's the key, you're building upon your credit history while paying for everyday expenses while earning cash or travel rewards all at the same time. The cash is literally "free" money earned for using the credit card. You can then apply the cash earned from purchases toward the repayment of the credit card balance, which essentially reduces your purchases. Most major credit cards offer somewhere between 3% to 5% cashback incentive on all purchases and offer additional cash back on select purchases. Typically, these special purchases vary from month to month. For example, one month the additional cashback incentive may apply toward gas purchases. The next month it may be applicable on grocery purchases, and maybe restaurant purchases the following month. Again, if these items are something that you would normally consume, not only does it make sense but you also gain more purchasing power by using your credit card since you're earning additional reward points or cash bonus. Greater bang per buck spent.

✓ *Pay off Balance Immediately*

It is pertinent that you make a payment on the credit card immediately. You can log into your credit card company's website and make payment online, free of charge. The key is to pay the entire balance before the next billing cycle. This will prevent interest charges on your purchases. Many people have found themselves paying more in interest than the actual items purchased as a result of carrying the balance over multiple billing cycles. Never opt to pay the minimum amount due. This is a major pitfall in using a credit card and we certainly want to avoid this misuse all together as the results are disastrous.

✓ *Is Credit a Smart Choice?*

Yes. Here's why using credit cards are a smart choice. You are maximizing your purchasing power. When you consider the average interest earned on cash deposits in a saving's account, on average, the interest paid to the account holder is about 2% to 3%. When you use your credit card, you're earning the same cash back and more on select purchases. Clearly, you have to make a purchase to get the interest and rewards; however, there are plenty of advantages. Earning travel rewards is also another advantage of using credit cards. If you enjoy travel, you can apply earned points towards flights for domestic or international destinations. Travel rewards can also be used for hotel lodging. My husband and I are always excited to view our reward balance earned and redeem for cash to use on our family vacations. In a nutshell, you are getting paid to use your credit card and earning a higher return than cash in your savings. Also, if you're a couple, using a joint credit card on groceries, gas, utilities and household items will allow you to earn more points sooner.

✓ *Take Advantage of Technology*

In this modern tech savvy era, we all have smart phones, tablets, laptops and other web enabled devices. If you think about it, you almost have your very own personal assistant with such devices. Incorporate this modern technology to assist with credit card monitoring. You can download your credit card company's app, set alerts as reminders to schedule payment, set up auto draft from your primary checking account, all with mobile gadgets. I recall buying a pair of earrings, during my undergraduate days, for less than $10 and having to repay almost $60 a few months later because I left the country to study abroad, and forgot to make the payment. Issuing personal checks and dealing with the hassle of postage or standing in line to make payment is almost a thing of the pass. You can access these services at the touch of a finger anywhere in the world. Optimize the use of these tools to help assist with financial goals. Technology has simplified our lives for the better in many aspects.

UNDERSTANDING INTEREST IMPACT

There are two types of interest, simple and compounded. **Simple interest** is a one-time interest charge applied to the principle. **Compounded interest** is applied for multiple periods, typically monthly, thus causing your balance to grow tremendously if left unpaid. For example, take a balance of $100 accruing simple interest of 10%; this result in a final balance of $110 since interest is only added once. With compound interest, which continuously adds the interest to the principle, the $100 balance becomes $110 at the end of the period, which can be daily. The 10% then gets accrued to this new principle, which now becomes $121, which then grows to $133 during the next compounding period. We can see how quickly the principle grows exponentially with compounding interest. You want to repay your balance in full to avoid the accrual of interest charges, especially compounded interest.

Interest is commonly referred to as Annual Percent Rate, or APR. Another term associated with credit cards is the Effective

Annual Interest Rate, also known as EAR. You may have noticed these terms reflected on credit card promotions or a billing statement. I want to take a minute to explain the differences between the two terms, which will allow you to make informed decisions when researching or comparing credit cards.

✓ *Annual Percentage Rate and Effective Interest Rate*

Annual percentage rate is the most common way to refer to interest and is expressed as a percentage per year. The APR captures all the cost and fees applicable for borrowing money over a year's time, and is standardized across banking institutions for credit cards. The *effective interest rate* includes inflation and compounding and is, therefore, the real cost of borrowing. With this information, APR is an easier method to use to compare credit cards fees since it's a standard measure. Then, look at the effective interest rate to get a picture of the real cost to you.

✓ *Retail Discount Cards*

Retail discount cards can also leave you with extra money in your pockets. They offer additional savings and benefits, and often can be combined with manufactures coupons. Simply shop and present your card to the cashier during checkout for saving. There is no charge or fee for the discount card. Some retailers may offer a store credit card to receive additional discounts, be wary of these offers as annual fees and interest usually will apply. Ask these questions up front. I would strongly caution to limit these retail credit cards, especially if there are annual fees incurred as a card holder and stick to one major credit card as explained earlier.

Chapter IV....... BUYING VERSUS RENTING A HOME

At some point, each and every one of us will come to a fork in life's road when we decide if we'll rent or buy our place of residency. Whether you live in an apartment, condo, duplex, townhome, or single home, each dwelling will incur property tax and a mortgage payment. When it's time to answer the question of buying versus renting, here are some of the factors you should keep in mind:

✓ *Things to Consider when Deciding*

If you choose to rent an apartment or a house, the mortgage on the property still has to be paid. As a renter, you are simply paying the mortgage payment for the owner of the property in the form of monthly rental expense. If the mortgage has been paid in full, the rental expense becomes straight profit for the landlord. Why not use this same allocation of money spent on rent to pay off your own real estate?

✓ *Renting in the Interim or Short-term*

I am a proponent of renting with a short-term horizon in mind. For most college students and young adults, renting your first apartment or condo is the logical road of progression. Most young people are exploring life, beginning new career opportunities, or simply trying to determine what their passion is. As a college student and young professional, I recall moving about four or five times, and that was just the norm. It's the best time in your life when you can pick up and move across town, out of state, or abroad! However, as we become more established, we want to begin to develop the mindset of "ownership."

✓ *Big Financial Obligation*

The most important aspect of purchasing a home is to set a budget, and stick to it! Not to be taken lightly, owning a home is a huge responsibility and financial obligation. There is typically a large initial investment in the form of the down payment, closing costs and yearly property taxes. The good news is that certain expenses are tax deductible, such as mortgage interest and property taxes. When considering buying a home, it's best to begin to save for a down payment toward the purchase of the home. The bigger the down payment, the lower the monthly mortgage payments will be, since the face value of the loan amount will be less. Simply stated, the more money you have saved toward the purchase of the home, the less you will have to borrow from the bank. Most mortgage lenders recommend home buyers to put down at least 20 percent of the cost of the home, which is a significant amount of money. Lenders view this as the homeowner's investment into their new home. Often, you'll have a lower interest rate offered by the lender if you can make a higher initial payment.

✓ *Private Mortgage Insurance*

Private mortgage insurance, known as PMI, is required by lenders for any down payment less than 20 percent, which is very common. Essentially, the PMI payments will be rolled into your mortgage payments. PMI fees are generally between 0.3 percent and 1.15 percent of the loan amount, which is paid as an annual premium.

Here's an example: Let's assume the purchase price of the home is $180,000 and you have saved 5 percent or $9,000 for the down payment. You will need to finance the remaining $171,000 in the form of a mortgage loan. Since the down payment is less than 20 percent, PMI is required. We will assume the annual premium is .45 percent, which the mortgage insurer calculates by multiplying .0045 by the loan amount of $171,000. This equates to an annual premium of $769.50 which amounts to 12 monthly payments of $64.13. The good news is that these payments have been tax deductible in the past. Keep tract of the payments as PMI can be discontinued once you've paid 80 percent of the home's original value.

✓ *Incentive and Special Programs*

If you are a first time home buyer this may seem a bit daunting, don't be dismayed if saving 20 percent towards a home seems out of reach. There are many special programs for homebuyers. Federal Housing Administration (FHA) mortgage loan is one such program that is a government-insured loan that offers low down payments, as well as lower rates. The FHA loan has many advantages such as a required down payment of only 3.5 percent, making it a viable option for many borrowers. My husband and I went with this option when we purchased our first home. Other programs that may be useful when house hunting include: Zero Down Payment Act, American Dream Down Payment Assistant and Habitat for Humanity. It's important to do your research first. Family, friends and co-workers who are homeowners are always great resources.

There are numerous advantages of owning your home. One of the biggest advantages of home ownership is that real estate generally appreciates over time. As a result, homeowners begin to build equity in their home. ***Home Equity*** is the difference between the outstanding loan amount and the fair market value of the house. As the loan balance is reduced as payments are made, the equity increases as the value of the property increases. Homeowners can earn a hefty profit from the equity accumulated during resell of the home, particularly in a strong housing market.

On another note, once your home is paid off, it is yours! You own it! You can raise your family in it, make it your retirement home, leave it to your children, donate it to a charity, sell it, or use it as an income property. Whatever you decide, you have the power and choice!

Chapter V ...... MORTGAGE AMORTIZATION SCHEDULE

Now that we're discussed the benefits of home ownership, I want to explain how interest accrues on a mortgage and how to avoid paying thousands of dollars in interest. Understanding a mortgage amortization schedule will help to demonstrate how to accomplish this savings. Making additional or accelerated payments toward your mortgage will result in early repayment, which ultimately saves huge bucks in the end.

During the early years of repayment of the loan, the majority of mortgage payments are applied directly toward interest, little goes toward actually reducing the principle. Making additions payments over the life of the loan will allow you to repay the loan early and save thousands of dollars in interest cost. Ensuring the extra payments goes toward the principal balance, instead of the interest payment, is very important. It may be necessary to call your mortgage bank or write a letter to specify that the additional payments are to be applied directly toward the balance, and not held for the next payment period. Often times, additional payments are held and applied to the next mortgage payment, which we want to avoid.

I can recall opening our mortgage statement at the end of our first year and being in disbelief. I was aware that the bulk of payments were applied to interest charged by the bank. However, it wasn't until I actually had my own mortgage payments that it really hit home. Wow! After a year of twelve monthly payments, we had barely reduced the principle balance on the loan. This was probably the most eye opening revelation for me. Like so many others, we were following the common repayment routine practiced by more than 95% of Americans, according to the FDIC. Let's see how we can change those statistics.

An ***amortization schedule*** is used to show the balance of a loan, the payments and interest owed over the life of the loan. I have created an amortization schedule using an Excel spreadsheet which will calculate the monthly payments and outstanding principle based upon the different payment scenarios and input. The results will be reflected in the following tables. We'll use the following loan terms: 30 years fixed mortgage, interest rate of 6% and loan amount of $180,000 for the first example of our home purchase. We will alter the payment amounts and frequencies to show how these changes impact the remaining loan balance and repayment schedule. Figure 1 summarizes the terms.

Figure 1

LOAN SUMMARY	
PRINCIPLE	$180,000
INTEREST RATE	6%
TERM (YEARS)	30

The first scenario assumes the homeowners are paying the minimum monthly payments due. Therefore, we have 360 payments over 30 years to satisfy our loan payoff. As reflected in Table 1 below, the interest paid over the life of the loan is approximately $208,509 and exceeds the original loan amount. Remember, the interest is solely the cost of borrowing money from the lender. From these results, we can conclude that it costs more to borrow money

18

from the lender than the actual purchase amount of the home. The real cost of borrowing a 30 year loan without making any additional payments is $388,509, which is the overall total repayment amount.

Table 1: Minimal Monthly Payments

Scenario 1: Minimal Monthly Payments	
Number of Monthly Payments	360
Number of Yearly Payments	30
Monthly Payment Amount	$1,079
Total Interest Paid	$208,509
Total Principal Paid	$180,000
Total Prepayments	$0
Total Paid	$388,509

If you're thinking, "That's a lot of money to pay in interest cost in itself," you are absolutely right. How can we reduce the interest payment? We'll start by examining scenario 2 shown in Table 2. Here's an example of how interest cost is reduced by making an extra payment per year toward the principal balance. Not only can we save thousands of dollars in interest, but it allows us to pay off the loan early. Let's see how much we'll save and the timeframe it will take to pay off the loan.

Table 2: Extra Payment per Year

Scenario 2: Extra Payment Per Year	
Number of Monthly Payments	297
Number of Yearly Payments	25
Monthly Payment Amount	$1,079
Total Interest Paid	$166,247
Total Principal Paid	$154,095
Total Prepayments	$25,901
Total Paid	$346,242

By making an additional payment per year, beginning at the end of first full year of repayment, we reduced interest from $208,509 in scenario 1, to $166,247 in scenario 2, a whopping savings of $42,262. Also, the loan will be repaid five years sooner. Overall, the prepayments of $25,901 reduced total payments from $388,509 to $346,242, a total savings of $42,267. Think of what you could do with the additional savings. I'm sure you can name a million and one things!

As stated earlier, the sooner we reduce the principle the less we incur in interest expense since the interest percentage is derived from the total principal balance. To validate this concept, let's assume we were financial able to apply the total prepayment in scenario 2 for $25,901 as a lump sum one year after the loan had been established. After updating the amortization schedule with the lump sum prepayment of $25,901, we get the following results reflected in Table 3; demonstrating the impact from making a large lump sum payment at the beginning of the loan.

Table 3: Total Lump Sum Prepayment Applied Early

Scenario 3: Same total Prepayment Paid Early	
Number of Monthly Payments	257
Number of Yearly Payments	21
Monthly Payment Amount	$1,079
Total Interest Paid	$122,497
Total Principal Paid	$154,097
Total Prepayments	$25,901
Total Paid	$302,495

The repayment period is further reduced from to 297 months to 257 months, or 21 years to repay the mortgage. This translates to an additional savings of $43,749 in interest expense when compared to the previous example. This demonstrates the significance of reducing the balance in the beginning of the prepayment period. By using the exact same total prepayment amount, and applying it all at once early on, we drastically reduce our loan repayment term and interest incurred.

In scenario 4, we will take a look at what a mere $100 per month translates to in terms of savings. As discussed in the chapter *"Spenders vs Savers,"* many of us may not look at the big picture when we're spending. Or, perhaps we have a misconception of the real impact of what may seem to be insignificant spending. Therefore we may not think that making an additional payment of $100 per month will have any influence on reducing our balance; however, that is further from the truth. You will be surprised to see how huge of an impact such a small monthly payment has in the long run. Data in Table 4 has been updated to reflect scenario 4. Let's take a look at the long term impact of making a small payment of $100 per month on a 30 year loan.

Table 4: Extra Payment of $100 per Month

Scenario 4: Extra Payment of $100 Per Month	
Number of Monthly Payments	289
Number of Yearly Payments	24
Monthly Payment Amount	$1,079
Total Interest Paid	$160,619
Total Principal Paid	$151,195
Total Prepayments	$28,800
Total Paid	$340,614

In Table 4, we can determine that paying an additional $100 per month toward the principle balance allows us to shave off 6 years from our 30 year loan. We will have the loan repaid in 24 years by sticking to this payment routine.

For those of you who are striving to be more a bit more aggressive, and have the financial means to do so, we'll examine how to pay off a 30 year $180,000 loan in just 15 years. Scenario 5 will illustrate how this can be achieved. Let's assume we are able to make an extra payment of $500 per month. Our amortization schedule has been updated to reflect an additional $500 per payment period applied toward the original $180,000 loan balance beginning with the first month.

Table 5: Extra Payment of $500 per Month

Scenario 5: Extra Payment of $500 Per Month	
Number of Monthly Payments	170
Number of Yearly Payments	14
Monthly Payment Amount	$1,079
Total Interest Paid	$87,160
Total Principal Paid	$95,499
Total Prepayments	$84,500
Total Paid	$267,158

From the results, we can conclude that an additional $500 payment will allow you to repay the 30 year loan in less than half the term period. The loan will be repaid in just 14 years, one year sooner than our target goal. Comparing this scenario to the original example in scenario 1, we have saved approximately $121,349 in interest expense alone.

Our final amortization example is the most accelerated and aggressive repayment schedule. Scenario 6 assumes an additional payment equating to the monthly mortgage amount, will be made each month. This may be the case for a married couple who are both generating income, and perhaps a promotion resulted in more household income. They have a short-term financial goal to eliminate the mortgage payments as soon as possible in order to pay off the house and free up cash for other opportunities. Here's what we find in Table 6 after updating the schedule.

Table 6: Extra Payment per Month

Scenario 6: Extra Payment Per Month	
Number of Monthly Payments	109
Number of Yearly Payments	9
Monthly Payment Amount	$1,079
Total Interest Paid	$53,486
Total Principal Paid	$63,446
Total Prepayments	$116,553
Total Paid	$233,484

Nearly 21 years are shaved off the original 30 year repayment schedule by doubling the payments per month and applying the second payment directly toward the principal, while drastically reducing interest cost. With this strategy, the mortgage will be paid off in 9 years! The total repayment cost will be roughly $233,000 compared to $389,000 in our first example in scenario 1.

To summarize, the examples began with the least aggressive repayment approach in scenario 1, and ended with the most aggressive repayment timeframe in scenario 6, which doubled the monthly payment amount. All six scenarios demonstrate and validate the impact that interest expense has on a home mortgage loan. The longer the loan term, the greater length of time the interest expense has to accrue. The larger the principle balance, the larger the percentage of interest charged. Making an additional payment towards the principle balance will exponentially reduce the years on the loan term and the overall cost to you, the homeowner.

Chapter VI .... PAYING OFF AUTO LOANS

When addressing auto loans, I do not place the same emphasis on making additional monthly payment as in the case of a mortgage loan. Making additional payments may deplete your cash savings, and the tradeoff isn't significant in terms of savings. Instead, my recommendation is to make the regular timely payments that result in the vehicle being paid off in 5 years. The key is to keep your car for at least 3 to 5 years after it has been completely paid off. This may seem a bit contradictory to the strategy for repaying your mortgage debt, so let me further explain.

Unlike real estate which, all things being equal, appreciates over time, the value of your vehicle actually depreciates once it leaves the car lot. The average car loan is typically less than $30,000 for most middle income families. Therefore, due to the much shorter term of the auto loan, which is generally 5 years, and the loan amount, I would not suggest making additional payments if the tradeoff will result in having less available funds for savings and investing. Remember, we must keep our overall financial health in mind when making these decisions.

If we use the amortization schedule introduced earlier and modify it to analyze the repayments of the auto loan, we can determine the real cost of borrowing, including interest. Let's assume we have a 5 year auto loan at 6% annual interest rate. We will borrow $25,000 to cover the cost of the car. Keep in mind that the interest rate charged by the bank can vary considerably, based on individual credit history. The table below summarizes our loan terms.

AUTO LOAN SUMMARY	
LOAN TERM (YEARS)	5
LOAN TERM (MONTHS)	60
ANNUAL RATE	6%
MONTHLY RATE	0.005
PRINCIPLE	$ 25,000
MONTHLY PAYMENT	$ 483.32

We'll examine a few scenarios on repaying auto loans by altering the frequency of payment and loan amounts. The monthly payment on the $25,000 loan at 6% for 5 years is $483.32. To begin, our first scenario assumes no additional payments will be made.

Table 1: Minimum Monthly Payments

Scenario 1: Minimal Monthly Payments	
Number of Monthly Payments	60
Number of Yearly Payments	5
Monthly Payment Amount	$483
Total Interest Paid	$3,997
Total Principal Paid	$25,000
Total Prepayments	$0
Total Paid	$28,997

By sticking to the monthly payment amount of $483, the loan will be repaid in 5 years and incur roughly $4,000 in interest expense. Our total repayment, after satisfying the cost of the loan, is nearly $29,000.

Let's move on to the next example and take a look at scenario 2, below. An additional payment per year will be made on the car loan. From our data, the addition payment results in the repayment of the loan in 4 years and six months. The total interest expense is $434 less than the prior example in scenario 1.

Table 2: Extra Payment per Year

Scenario 2: Extra Payment Per Year	
Number of Monthly Payments	55
Number of Yearly Payments	4.6
Monthly Payment Amount	$483
Total Interest Paid	$3,563
Total Principal Paid	$22,583
Total Prepayments	$2,417
Total Paid	$28,563

The prepayments allowed the loan to be paid off a few months early totaled $2,417, bringing our total repayment to $28,563, a difference of $434 when compared to total amount paid in scenario 1. Before arriving at a final conclusion, let's examine the third scenario reflected in Table 3. Our last example assumes we are in a financial position to make an additional payment every six months. The question we need to ask ourselves is, "Should we make additional payments or, would the additional payments be maximized elsewhere?"

Table 3: Extra Payment per 6 Months

Scenario 3: Extra Payment Per 6 Months	
Number of Monthly Payments	52
Number of Yearly Payments	4
Monthly Payment Amount	$483
Total Interest Paid	$3,415
Total Principal Paid	$21,615
Total Prepayments	$3,383
Total Paid	$28,413

Essentially, in financial terms, what's our opportunity cost? Before we answer these questions, let's look at the results. The loan will be repaid in a little over four years. Our total interest expense is $3,415, the early prepayments totaled $3,383 and the total repayment amount was $28,413.

✓ *Opportunity Cost*

Comparing scenario 1 in which we made no additional payments to the last example, in which we made payments every six months, our savings obtained from making the additional early payments was only $584 ($28,997-$28,413). However, cash outflow, in the form of prepayments, exceeded $3,000. This is our *opportunity cost* which simply means what we forego or give up to make an alternative action. In the case of both scenario 2 and 3, by making additional payments, the opportunity cost is foregoing the use of cash for other benefits, such as earning interest by investing it elsewhere.

Although the additional payments allowed us to repay the car sooner than the 5 year term, the financial benefit did not substantiate the use of cash that could have been contributed toward an emergency fund or invested. To answer the question of whether we should make additional payments toward the auto loan repayment, the data concludes that additional payments does not present the most optimal opportunity for cost savings.

✓ *Keep the Vehicle a Few Years after Paying it Off*

Unlike the longer-term, home mortgage loan which undoubtedly results in massive savings in the tens of thousands of dollars when paid off early, the maximum value of the auto loan is not gained by early repayment. Instead, it's realized by keeping the vehicle after it's paid off in full and the title has been transferred from the bank to you. You are now the rightful owner of the vehicle. Thus, what was once your liability to the bank now becomes your asset.

To capitalize on your vehicle, hold your car for a minimum of 3 to 5 years and continue to make the same monthly car payments of $483, only this time, pay yourself instead of the bank! After 3 years, you will have saved $17,400 which increases to $29,000 after 5 years; enough to buy a brand new car while eliminating the need to finance if you chose to. Ultimately, it boils down to individual desires and preferences. I'm well aware that many people like to have the latest and greatest model of vehicles. Here's one of my favorite sayings, "If it isn't broken, don't fix it." By keeping your car for a few years, you'll amass huge savings by foregoing a car note. Less money out, means more money in!

Chapter VII .... INVESTMENT VEHICLES

In this chapter, I want to discuss several investment vehicles or options that many of you may not be familiar with. About eight years ago I ventured out of the box and invested in a financial product known as a Certificate of Deposit. So what exactly is a Certificate of Deposit (CDs) and how do they work as an investment option?

✓ *Certificate of Deposits*

CDs are one of the safest investment options and an excellent choice to reach your financial goals. CDs are a deposit account offered by a banking institution or thrift and yield a higher interest return than a traditional savings account. CDs are backed by the government through the Federal Deposit Insurance Corporation (FDIC) up to $250,000. Banks issues both short-term and long-term cds. A short-term cd could mature in 6 months or a year, while a long-term cd could mature in 5, 10 or 20 years. There is a known fixed interest rate that will be paid on your deposit in intervals or at the end of the investment period.

Let's assume you have $5,000 that you will not need access to for at least a year. Therefore, you would like to invest in a one year cd. The bank guarantees a 6% return at the end of the year. You would deposit $5,000 to invest in the cd and the bank will disburse $5,300 to you at the end of the year, upon maturity. This is the total of your original deposit plus $300 earned in interest as a result of lending unused money to the bank for one year. CDs offer a higher return than a traditional checking or savings account. My husband and I chose this option to meet our financial goals and budget for our wedding expenses. We planned to marry in two years and knew we wanted to choose an investment option that was risk free. We also considered when payments would come due and took into consideration when we would need access to our money to pay for venues, honeymoon, etc. With those factors in mind, we chose a short-term 1 year cd.

Overall, cds offer a safe, flexible, risk-free strategy for investing excess cash to meet targeted short term and long term financial goals such as planning for a wedding, saving up to purchase a home or buying a new car. The alternative of simply sitting in a traditional checking or saving account, which earns minimum interest on the balance, is unattractive by far. Because cds are secured by the FDIC, there is an additional peace of mind that is gained knowing that if the banking institution encounters any solvency issues; your investment is still secured.

✓ *401k Retirement Plan*

Another great way to invest into your future is via a 401k Plan. A 401k plan allows employees to contribute pretax dollars into a retirement account. Most companies also offer 100% matching on your contributions up to a certain threshold. The key is to contribute the maximum amount per pay period for which your company will match. Your company's match to your contribution is free money folks! Here's how it works. Let's assume your company offers employees 5% matching of pre-tax earnings, your base salary is $50K per year, and you receive a pay check on a bi-monthly basis. This means you should contribute $961.54 per week or roughly $1,923.08 every two weeks to your 401K plan and your company will then match your contribution amount, giving you a total of $3,846.16. Young people especially, this is the perfect time to take advantage of this opportunity. The more time the funds have to grow, the greater your retirement savings will be when you need them most. However, it's never too late to start contribution to your company's plan if you haven't.

✓ *Public Stocks*

One of the main concepts in finance is the **risk-return tradeoff** theory. Simply stated, the higher the risk, the higher the return, and, thus, the introduction of the stock market. Investing in the stock market offers tremendous potential growth coupled with high returns of invested dollars. The risk is the volatility that occurs in the stock market which could result in huge loss of money you've invested if unfavorable, or huge gains if favorable. The key is to have a diversified portfolio. *Diversification* simply means having a mix of stocks within different sectors to help improve overall performance. You may want to have a mix of technology, pharmaceutical, research, retail, energy, social media and restaurant stocks, as an example. This will allows you to gain from well performing stocks while reducing the loss on the stock that may not be performing well due to market conditions or adverse news impacting a particular sector.

Some of you may be interested in investing in the public stock market but may not know how to get started. That was my dilemma. Ironically, I had studied renowned option pricing and dividend theories such as Black Scholes Model, Dividend Discount and other investment strategies as an undergraduate finance major at Penn Start University. I still didn't quite know how to get started investing for myself once I began working. A lot of the hesitation was probably just the fact that I still didn't know if I could afford it. As a student, we had always practiced stock trading with huge balances, so I sort of had the perception that investing in the public market was only accessible to high net worth individuals. Definitely not true.

The great news is that the popularity of online trading has created a sense of accessibility and affordability to the average investor, including myself. Brokerage firms such as Scottrade, TDAmeritrade, and E-Trade have huge online presence which has resulted in relatively low fees and transactional costs. You can open an account for as low as $1,000 and place trades to buy or sell shares of publicly traded stocks for a fee of $7, on average. I've found online trading to be extremely user friendly, with many companies having local branches and 24 hour chat and or phone assistance to answer trading questions.

I will encourage you to begin to build a portfolio of stocks using minimum excess funds. While I certainly would not recommend investing your mortgage payment, there are many stocks that are pretty stable and offer steady growth. There are also several simple investment strategies which allow you to limit the downside risk of buying and selling stocks. For example, you may want to buy 5 shares of Microsoft which have a market price of around $44. The *market price* is the current price the stock is trading at. Let's assume you believe the shares are overpriced by $2; therefore, you can place a limit order to buy at $42. A *limit order* allows you a guaranteed price if the trade is possible, therefore, it does not guarantee execution. If Microsoft shares fall to $42, the order to buy the 5 shares will be executed. On the other hand, if share price only falls to $43 or increases, the limit order to buy will not be executed or completed. The same method can be used to sell shares of stocks that you own. A similar order type is the *stop-on-quote* also known as stop-loss order, which guarantees execution of a trade, but does not guarantee the price. Stop-on-Quote is a good strategy to use on stocks you own but believe stock price will begin to fall over the long-run. For example, we owned shares of Alibaba (the largest Chinese ecommerce company) which reached $120 per share after the company went public. The company was faced with many lawsuits subsequently, causing the value of the shares to plummet. To limit the loss, we placed a stop-on-quote order to sell shares if price fell below $85. A few days later, share price did fall below $85 and the order was executed to sell the shares at the market price. Thus, we still were able to sell at a price higher then we brought and realize a gain.

These are a few order types and strategies that are very helpful when buying and selling stocks for your portfolio. Of course, you can always research additional topics pertaining to buying and selling stocks if you would like to gain more knowledge on this topic. Over time, you will become more comfortable with the idea of maintaining a portfolio of stocks. Many apps are available to download on your mobile device which allows you to monitor the performance of the companies you've invested in, or create a watch list of companies you may be interested in buying. *Yahoo Finance* is a great resource for researching the performance of a company, obtaining stock quotes and other current market data.

Each publicly traded company has a stock ticker symbol and is listed on one of the major stock exchanges. The top 5 major stock exchanges in the world are: The New York Stock Exchange, NASDAQ, Tokyo Stock Exchange, London Stock Exchange, and Shanghai Stock Exchange. Let's examine one of the most popular social media companies, as an example. Facebook is listed on the Nasdaq Stock Exchange. Using Yahoo Finance we can search Facebook's stock symbol, or ticker, and find that it's listed as FB and see its current share price. The chart below reflects the movement of Facebook's stock price over the period of a year.

Figure 1: Facebook- One of the most popular social media sites

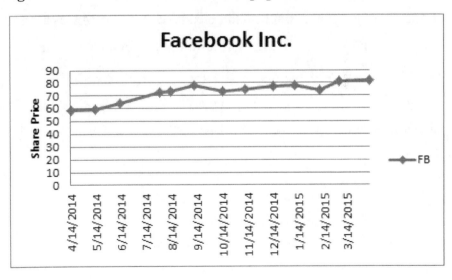

As you can see, the stock traded around $60 in April of 2014; a year later share price has steadily increased and has climbed over $80 per share. I have created a chart to show the price movement. However, if you were to search Yahoo Finance, it would create a similar chart for you. You can also select different time periods for which you would like to view the history of the stock's performance such as 1 day interval, 1 month, 1 year or 5 years. This is how easy it is to obtain information on the performance of any publicly traded company that you may be interested in. The internet has made this research as simple as a click of the finger. Here's my motto when it comes to taking on something new, "Sometimes you just have to muster up the courage, jump out of your comfort zone, and do it!"

❖ **Initial Public Offering**

Initial Public Offerings (IPOs) is when a company is first listed on one of the exchange markets and shares of their stock become available to the general public and investors to buy. 2014 was a great year for initial public offerings. According to Inc.com, the average returns were 16 percent, although the return was much higher in 2013, nearing 41 percent. In any fashion, double digit returns are still much higher than your traditional savings account.

Figure 2: Alibaba- Largest IPO in history

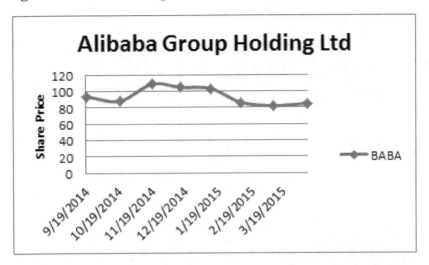

Alibaba, the largest ecommerce company in China had the largest IPOs in history raising $22 billion when it went public on the NYSE in September 2014. Unfortunately, the company has been hit with some legal issues since; as a result, share price has declined from its high of nearly $120 per share.

❖ *Stock Splits*

Apple announced a 7-for-1 stock split in June 2014. As a result, shareholders gained an additional six shares of stock. A *stock split* increases the number of shares and reduces the price per share but does not impact the market capitalization of the company. For example, prior to Apple's 7-for-1 split, if you wanted to own Apple in your portfolio it cost $700 to own a single share. After the split, shares were offered for $92.69 and Apple offered current investors 6 more shares to adjust their portfolio's value. Share price has climbed up to roughly $129 since the split and is reflected in figure 3 below.

Figure 3: Apple's 7-for-1 stock split

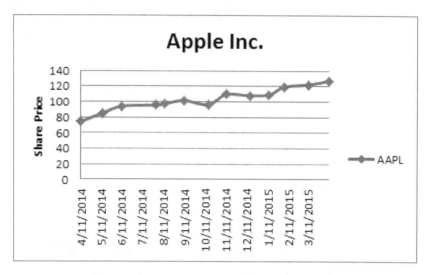

❖ **Mergers and Acquisitions (M&A)**

Kraft Foods recently announced it would merge with privately held company Heinz. In March 2015, the merge was official. Kraft-Heinz is expected to grow revenue while cutting cost. A **merger** is the formal joining of two separate companies, while an **acquisition** occurs when one company takes over the acquired or target company. We had discussed owning shares of Kraft, but never brought. To our dismay, shares soared by almost 30 percent immediately after the announcement was made. On the other hand, this merger resulted in huge returns for those that were previously invested in Kraft prior to the merge. Figure 4 shows stock price trading around $60- $65 per share prior to the merge in March, surging to $89 after joining with Heinz.

Figure 4: Kraft announces merger with Heinz

IPOs, stock splits, mergers and acquisitions are some of the notable events that can create great momentum in stock prices for publicly traded companies. While there is great potential for returns on an investment, there is also ample risk due to volatility of the stock market. That's just the nature of the market. However, there are many strategies to limit the downside risk, the easiest being diversification.

Chapter VIII............................ TIME VALUE OF MONEY

One concept relevant in any arena of finance, whether it be corporate, small business, government or personal finance, is **Time Value of Money**. In its most simplistic explanation, it simply states that a dollar today is worth more than a dollar received in the future because it can be invested today, earn interest, and be worth more than the dollar received later. Of course this depends on the interest earned. Time value of money provides an understanding of how money works and grows over time. It is a very valuable concept for managing personal finances because each one of us is responsible for financial decision making on an individual level. Once you grasp a solid understanding, you'll find it's a powerful tool for managing your money or making investment decisions. Without being too technical, if you're familiar with Excel spreadsheets, there is a built-in function which calculates many of these principles. However, I will present the formulas.

Almost all of us have made a series of fixed payments such as rent, mortgage, car loan or student loan payments. This outgoing cash flow is called an *annuity*. Annuities can also be fixed income coming in. For example, if you own a rental property and receive monthly payments, that's an annuity as well. If you're really lucky and win the lottery, you may receive fixed payments over time, which is an annuity. Time value of money is also used for more complex applications such as bond valuation and stock returns. There is a fundamental value in understanding the usefulness of this concept.

Two main principles of time value of money used in personal finance are Future Value and Present Value. We'll look at an example to better understand these principles. Let's assume you have $100 to invest today that will earn 12% interest. A year from now that $100 is now worth $112. If you wait to receive the $100 dollars a year from now, without having had invested it, it's only worth $89 adjusted for inflation. We'll see a bit later how this is calculated.

Future Value (FV)

The *Future Value* (FV) of a cash flow tells us how much money we would earn at some point of time in the future, with a known interest rate. There are two ways to calculate future value: simple annual interest and annual compound interest. *Simple annual interest* only earns interest on the amount you've invested, called the principal amount. *Compound interest* earns interest on both the principal as well as interest already earned. You can think of compound interest as earning "interest on interest." Compounded interest is the best scenario for earning potential on an investment, since the balance grows much faster than simple interest. In our initial example, the future value of $100 to be received in a year was $112. Because the investment period was just one year, both our simple and compounded calculation will results in the same return. Let's take a closer look.

Simple Annual Interest

$$FV = PV * ((1 + (r*t))$$

Where:

- PV= Present Value or Initial Investment
- r= Interest Rate
- t= Number of years

$$FV = \$100 * ((1 + (.12*1)))$$
$$FV = \$100 * ((1 + .12))$$
$$FV = \$112$$

We will now use the second method, annual compounded interest to calculate future value. Again, we will arrive at the same return due to the one year period.

Annual Compounded Interest

$$FV = PV(1 + r)^t$$

Where:

- PV=Present Value or Initial Investment
- r=annual compounded interest rate
- t=number of years

$$FV = \$100(1 + .12)^1$$
$$FV = \$100(1.12)^1$$
$$FV = \$112$$

Future Value (FV) using Simple Annual Interest & Annual Compound Interest:

Let's look at another example using a period greater than 1 year to see how our investment grows with compounding interest. We'll use the same variables in the following example but will compare the interest earned using simple and compounded annual interest.

Example 1-Simple Annual Interest

You invest $1,000 for five years with an interest rate of 10% and earn simple interest. The future value would be $1,500.

FV = PV *((1+ (r*t))
FV = $1,000 * ((1+ (.10*5))
FV = $1,000 * ((1+.5))
FV = $1,000 * (1.5)
FV = $1,500

This means after five years, your initial investment of $1,000 has earned a return of $500 in interest, equivalent to $100 per year. Not bad.

Now, let's take a look at an even more impressive return using compounded annual interest. Remember, compounded interest earns interest on the interest previously earned in addition to the initial investment.

Example 2-Compounded Annual Interest

You invest $1,000 for five years with an interest rate of 10% compounded annually. The future value is now roughly $1,610.

$$FV = PV(1 + r)^t$$
$$FV = \$1,000(1 + .10)^5$$
$$FV = \$1,000(1.10)^5$$
$$FV = \$1,610.51$$

With compounded interest, the initial investment of $1,000 has earned a return of $610 in interest during the five year investment period, equivalent to $122 per year. By earning compounded annual interest, an additional $22 per year is gained in comparison to the annual earnings gained with simple interest.

The best outcome to maximize earnings potential is to have frequent compounding periods. Some investments options offer semi-annual or quarterly compounding periods. To demonstrate the earning potential for an investment, let's compare the returns of simple interest paid annually versus compounded interest paid annually, semi-annual and quarterly.

Table 1: 5 Year Holding Period

@ 10%	Five Year Returns			
	Simple Interest	Annual Compound	Semi-Annual	Quarterly
$1,000	$1,500	$1,611	$1,629	$1,639
$5,000	$7,500	$8,053	$8,144	$8,193
$10,000	$15,000	$16,105	$16,289	$16,386
$15,000	$22,500	$24,158	$24,433	$24,579
$20,000	$30,000	$32,210	$32,578	$32,772

Table 2: 10 Year Holding Period

@ 10%	Ten Year Returns			
	Simple Interest	Annual Compound	Semi-Annual	Quarterly
$1,000	$2,000	$2,594	$2,653	$2,685
$5,000	$10,000	$12,969	$13,266	$13,425
$10,000	$20,000	$25,937	$26,533	$26,851
$15,000	$30,000	$38,906	$39,799	$40,276
$20,000	$40,000	$51,875	$53,066	$53,701

Table 3: 15 Year Holding Period

@ 10%	Fifteen Year Returns			
	Simple Interest	Annual Compound	Semi-Annual	Quarterly
$1,000	$2,500	$4,177	$4,322	$4,400
$5,000	$12,500	$20,886	$21,610	$21,999
$10,000	$25,000	$41,772	$43,219	$43,998
$15,000	$37,500	$62,659	$64,829	$65,997
$20,000	$50,000	$83,545	$86,439	$87,996

45

Table 4: 20 Year Holding Period

@ 10%	Twenty Year Returns			
	Simple Interest	Annual Compound	Semi-Annual	Quarterly
$1,000	$3,000	$6,727	$7,040	$7,210
$5,000	$15,000	$33,637	$35,200	$36,048
$10,000	$30,000	$67,275	$70,400	$72,096
$15,000	$45,000	$100,912	$105,600	$108,144
$20,000	$60,000	$134,550	$140,800	$144,191

❖ **HIGHLIGHTS:**

- We can invest any amount of money today and potentially earn interest. Therefore, a dollar today is worth more than a dollar to be received in the future, because of earning potential

- Compounding annual interest grows at a faster rate than simple annual interest

- The greater the number of compounding periods, the greater the return on the investment

- The longer the investment period, the more time funds have to accrue earned interest

- Time is an important factor in the equation for investing and cash flow

Present Value (PV)

Present Value tells us how much a cash flow received in the future is worth in today's dollars. In other words, how much money do I need today to receive a certain amount in the future? We used the present value concept to determine how much $100 to be received in a year is worth today, accounting for inflation. Using the PV formula, we determined that we would need to have $89 today invested at 12%

46

to get a return of $100 in a year. This means that an investor should pay no more than $89 today to receive $100 at 12% a year from now. If we pay more than $89, the investment is less attractive. Here is how we calculated the present value of a cash flow in our original TVM example above: PV=100/$(1 + .12)^1$ = $89

$$PV= \frac{CF}{(1+r)^t}$$

- PV=Present Value
- CF=Future Cash Flow
- r=interest rate or discount rate
- t=number of years

Why is the Present Value concept important?

Present value answers the question of "How much money will I need to invest today to have a specified amount in the future?" Of course, we have to use a known interest rate. Present value is used in corporate finance to determine pension obligations, bond yields, and spot rates of commodities, currencies and other securities, just to put into context its value.

Understanding the present value concept will assist us when planning for long term personal financial goals. For example, if you want to purchase a car for $25,000 in 5 years you would use present value to calculate how much you need to deposit today, at a known interest rate, to grow to $25,000 when you are ready to buy that new car!

Let's use Present Value formula to find out how much we would need today to buy that car when we are ready.

Using the PV formula above:

Example 1

$$PV = \frac{\$25,000}{(1+.12)^5}$$

$$PV = \frac{\$25,000}{(1.12)^5}$$

$$PV = \frac{\$25,000}{1.76}$$

PV=$14,185.67

We were able to determine that we will need to invest $14,186 at 12% to accrue to $25,000 in five years. In financial terms, we would say that the present value of $25,000 is $14,185.67 at 12% interest rate. How great is this concept! We can see how valuable time value of money principles are in our everyday financial decision making. Of course, we have to consider inflation.

Example 2

Let's assume you want to purchase a building in order grow your business venture in 10 years. How much would you need to invest today if you want to have $200,000 to buy the building? Assuming the interest rate per year is 10%, we have:

$$PV = \frac{\$200,000}{(1+.10)^{10}}$$

$$PV = \frac{\$200,000}{(1.10)^{10}}$$

$$PV = \frac{\$200,000}{2.59}$$

PV= $77,108.66

You'll need to have $77,108.66 to deposit into an account earning 10% interest per year for ten years to secure a future value of $200,000 to purchase your office building. In other words, $77,108.66 is the present value of $200,000 in ten years earning 10% interest. Hopefully, you are feeling more comfortable from the various scenarios and examples presented. Although I've dedicated a chapter on home ownership and early payoff of mortgage loans, let's assume you'd opt not to finance your loan but would rather save, to pay cash up front. For our final example, perhaps you've just graduated college and would like to be a homeowner in 10 years. Once again, we'll pull out the powerful model of present value.

Example 3

You plan to save for ten years to purchase a home and would like to know how much money you need to put away in an account. Your budget is $225,000 and interest is 12% per year.

$$PV = \frac{\$225{,}000}{(1 + .12)^{10}}$$

$$PV = \frac{\$225{,}000}{(1.12)^{10}}$$

$$PV = \frac{\$225{,}000}{3.11}$$

PV=$72,443.98

There, we have our answer! The present value of $225,000 in 10 years at 12% interest is $72,444. This means we will need $72,444 today if we want our money to grow to $225,000 in 10 years at the given interest. Having a financial goal is great, but understanding how to get there is even better!

Hopefully, the various practical scenarios used as examples gave you a better understanding of annuities, future value and present value concepts. You can incorporate the time value of money principles into your personal or small business finances to help you make sound financial decisions. I hope you feel more educated and empowered to aim for, but more importantly, achieve your financial goals, both short-term and long-term.

Chapter IX.............................. LIFE INSURANCE

Unfortunately, I've experienced the tragedy of losing a loved one unexpectedly. My father was tragically killed when I was a teenager. This horrific incident left my mother a single parent of five children. Sadly, he had canceled his insurance policy a few months prior to his death. The financial burden left on a family who has lost a loved one without adequate life insurance is overwhelming. Too many families can relate to similar experiences and coming together to raise funds, just to give a proper memorial and burial. No one should have to experience this heartache. We can all be proactive to ensure we are not contributing to this dilemma by providing financial security through a life insurance policy.

Having life insurance gives you and your loved ones a peace of mind. It reduces the stress of wondering how, and if, they will be able to keep the lights on, pay the bills and afford their children's education? That's the peace of mind gained by owning a life insurance policy. Life insurance ensures your loved ones, who rely on you for financial support, will be taken care of when you are deceased. They will be able to maintain their quality of living.

No parent wants to think of the unimaginable grief of losing a child. Every parent's prayer for their child is to be happy, healthy, and outlive them. The reality is, the unthinkable happens and sadly, many parents will experience the anguish of burying their child. Having a policy for your child will cover any unpaid medical bills in the event that the child was ill or given medical care before passing.

The life insurance policy will pay for funeral expenses and relieve the financial burden of the unexpected related expenses.

A life insurance policy for your child can also provide savings for their future. That's because certain whole life insurance policies build cash value over time and can be cashed out when the child reaches a certain age, if they so choose. Some plans double the initial coverage amount at age 18. Premiums are locked in and never change as long as premiums are paid on time, even into adulthood. The coverage amount can be increased when the child becomes an adult. Gerber's Grow-Up Plan is an example of a whole life policy which builds cash value.

✓ *Types of Insurance Coverage*

There are generally two types of life insurance policies: term insurance or cash value insurance. ***Term Life Insurance*** provides coverage for a specific period or term which is typically for five, ten, fifteen or twenty years. It pays a death benefit only if the insured were to die in the term of the coverage period. After the term ends, so too does the coverage. Term insurance does not accumulate any cash value. It does typically offer the highest protection for the amount of premium paid. However, each time you renew the policy the premium increases. *Cash Value Insurance* can be one of several types: Whole Life Insurance, Universal Life Insurance and Variable Life Insurance. Now, we'll examine the cash value options. ***Whole Life Insurance*** provides coverage for the duration of life; as long as the premiums are paid, which are typically fixed. Premiums can be much higher for the same amount of term insurance when the policy

52

is initially drafted. In the long run, the premiums become smaller than the premiums you would pay if you continued to renew a term policy for the same coverage amount. The cash value offered varies between policies; therefore you would need to inquire about cash accumulation per policy. *Universal Life Insurance* is a flexible policy that allows you to vary your premium payments and the amount of coverage. There is also a component of the policy that allows you to earn interest on the premiums paid. On the other hand, if the annual premium and interest earned is less than the charges, your account value will become lower and could eventually end coverage. To prevent that, you may need to increase your premium payments or reduce your coverage amount. *Variable Life Insurance* death benefits and the cash value depend on the investment performance of a separate account(s), which could be invested in mutual funds or other investment vehicles in accordance with policy regulations. Under this type of insurance, you will have higher death benefits and cash value if the investments component performs well.

✓ *Shopping for Insurance*

So, how do you shop for life insurance? Here are three steps to keep in mind when comparing plans: First, determine the amount of coverage you will need, and more importantly, be sure it fits within your budget. Ensure the premiums due on the coverage will be affordable. Many policyholders have lost coverage because they were unable to maintain the monthly premiums, resulting in a policy lapse. Be sure that both the premium and coverage amount makes sense for you. Second, choose the type of life insurance policy that best meet your needs. Consider your age, health, any family members who rely on you for financial support such as children, parents, siblings, etc. Lastly, make an informed decision after taking all factors into consideration. Never be afraid to address any questions or concerns with the insurance agent to ensure you have the best policy to meet your needs.

Chapter X.........PLANNING FOR A FAMILY

This should be one of the most exciting and joyful times in a couple's life. The anticipation of a little human being who will share your genetic composition enters into the world in just a few short months. Some of us immediately begin to guess the sex of the baby based upon how we're feeling, the profile of the baby bump, and some of us may even refer to old wives' tales! Next are the name games; what will we name our new bundle of joy? Will we give them our same initials? Will we name them after our parents, relatives or a dear friend? Will they have a biblical name such as Joshua or Joseph, or Mary, if it's a girl? Or, will you give them their own identity? These are some of the relatively fun and easier questions to answer.

A new baby should be one of the most exciting and anticipating times in our lives. Unfortunately, for many parents the thrill and excitement begins to transition to worry, distress and anxiety. The enormity of the emotional and financial responsibility begins to set in. For many new parents, the distress is a result of one's current financial situation. The tough questions begin to surface. Will we be able to provide for this new baby? Can we afford childcare? Can we afford healthcare? Can we afford to stay at home with the baby or will we have to work? Will we be able to maintain our livelihood? These are some of the concerns that many parents have when expecting an addition.

While I can assure you I don't have all the answers to calm your worries about being a new parent, I can offer some financial advice that will drastically reduce them. The purpose of this chapter is to teach you how to eliminate financial stress and maintain your livelihood when starting a family. Fortunately, we were able to plan ahead before having our daughter and, as a result, I was able to step away from my role in corporate treasury as a financial analyst to be a full-time stay at home mom to our daughter. We had always been avid travelers prior to starting a family and have been fortunate to maintain that lifestyle as a result of planning, and are even more grateful to share the experiences with our baby girl.

My conviction in writing this chapter is to share, with anyone and everyone, how we were able to continue our standard of living without the financial worries many people experience. I believe we were created by God to share our experiences to help empower others, and let them know they too can achieve success. I particularly feel a sense of responsibility, as a minority, to reach out to my community to bring awareness to financial education and empowerment. One of my favorite quotes by the late Dr. Maya Angelou is, *"When you learn, teach, when you get, give."* With that said, here are a few tips:

> ➤ **Discuss Finances Together as a Partnership**

Here's the reality, if you are a couple who's planning to have a family or already have a family, the dynamics should instantly form a partnership in all aspects. Openly discussing and examining your finances, as a couple, is very important. It builds trusts between the two of you, and to a larger degree, eliminates financial fears because you are both informed about your financial status. Too often, there is the misconception of believing the male should not disclose their financial obligations to their spouse. Here's the misconception; a bill is due and is not paid on time, late fees are accrued and the balance due grows. Meanwhile, the wife is unaware and the husband believes as long as he does not reveal this financial hardship, everything will be ok. What will happen is that the financial stress of trying to be in charge and keep everything together will began to negatively manifest in the relationship. The bills will spiral out of control as they are not being paid and the relationship will be in turmoil.

The best rule of thumb to minimize financial stress is for couples to be transparent regarding finances, and engage in open conversations about their financial health. The power of two is a wonderful thing. Don't be afraid to lean on each other for support and financial decision-making as a team. It's a win-win outcome.

> **Practice Living on One Income**

Assuming there is a two income household, use the majority of the primary income to cover the largest monthly expenses. Typically, this will include your mortgage or rent. The secondary income will be used to cover the least expensive or remaining monthly expenses, such as utilities. This strategy of paying the bulk of the living expenses with one income, and saving the majority of the second, will maximize your long-term financial security and allow you to comfortably prepare for your new addition. If you are thinking, "Once we pay our monthly expenses, there isn't much money left to save." I would strongly challenge the two of you to really prioritize your needs, eliminate the majority of wants, and make a conscious effort to set aside savings to jump start your new beginnings.

> **Provide stability for yourself**

Before planning to have a family, evaluate where you are in life. Use this time as a reflection period to assess if you are in a position to take on the responsibility of providing and nurturing another human being who will be solely dependent on you. One of the most overwhelming experiences we can encounter is bringing another human being into the world without the financial, emotional or physical necessities to care for them. This is not to say that being new parents isn't overwhelming in itself.

Think about the basic necessities you'll need. Will you be able to afford them or will you need to rely on others for financial support? Do you have an established career? Will you be able to provide adequate housing for your new addition? These are some of the questions you want to seriously discuss with your spouse before having a family.

It's really difficult to put an exact figure on how much it costs to raise a child. The best advice I can offer is to consider what I discuss in the beginning of the book. Take an honest and hard look at your financial health using what you've learned thus far. Then, determine if you are ready to take the gigantic step of being a parent. If you are ready, it's a wonderful chapter in your life!

> **Work toward becoming homeowners**

Owning a home for the first time is exciting as well as an enormous responsibility. In many respects, it builds the foundation for stability in one's life. It is a safe haven, particularly when raising a family. Homeownership evokes a feeling of security for you and your family and gives children the confidence to thrive in other areas because of the strong symbolic foundation of stability. Providing a child with a home they can call their own is invaluable.

As parents, homeownership inspires a feeling of gratitude and pride knowing one day you'll be able to pass the house down to your children, if you choose. More importantly, it is a contributing factor for providing consistency in your child's upbringing while instilling values. From a financial perspective, not only are you creating lasting memories in your home but building equity over the years which benefit your family in the long run.

➢ Practice economical spending habits

This is the time to think about shifting your mindset in terms of spending habits. If you're a "spender, this is certainly the time to embrace cost-effective spending habits. Instead of buying the most expensive item, began to think about how you can obtain the greatest "bang per buck" on your dollar. In other words, get your money's worth.

You want to begin to think quality and functionality over brand recognition. Often times we pay a much higher premium on an item because of name recognition. I've seen this first hand when I was an cost accountant for a company that manufactured paint. Lowes was their largest customer. The only difference between customers paying $40 for a gallon of paint instead $20, was the brand label on the paint can. The content was exactly the same. I challenge you to begin to take a closer look at what you are paying for. If you can save 50% on an item and obtain the same quality and functionality, you will have more money in your pocket. Start with small everyday purchases. For example, instead of buying Tylenol brand the next time you have a headache, opt for the generic brand. You'll be surprised to know that by reading the labels, nine times out of ten, they will have the same active ingredients.

When you begin to apply this simple practice to every single purchase, overtime, it will become second nature. You'll learn how to value your money and how to avoid overpaying for items. More importantly, you'll end up saving lots of money on your purchases.

> **Prioritize necessities over wants**

Many of us can decipher the things we absolutely need on a daily basis versus the non-essential items we want. The key to prioritizing our needs from our wants is not being able to identify them; instead, it's being able to practice self-discipline which is instrumental. Recognizing our needs allows us to put things into perspective. Begin by asking yourself one simple question "Is this a necessity?" If you can honestly answer the question and not waiver if the answer is "no", you'll find yourself saving money. Being steadfast will help you to make other important decisions in your life. You'll be glad you made certain decisions to cut back on unnecessary spending. Once the new addition comes into the picture, you'll be able to put the saving to use immediately!

➢ Focus on educational and career objectives

I'll start by saying that it's never too late to pursue educational and career goals. Whenever anyone chooses to better their circumstances, by improving themselves in any capacity, it is certainly commendable.

What I'd like to offer from my experience in this journey of financial planning and parenthood is to pursue your education and career objectives prior to starting a family. Give it one hundred and ten percent. Once the time is right and you are ready to have a family it's no longer about you, but about your child. If you decide to take some time off from your career to stay at home with your baby, you're financially prepared. The stress of working long hours to provide for your family is not a factor. I've been where a lot of you are and know first-hand what it's like when you are trying to further your education, work long hours and balance being a wife, or a husband for that matter. It can be very challenging at times, but extremely rewarding in the end. You will be able to have more time and energy to focus on your family and enjoy life without the hustle and bustle of everything else.

Like many of us, there are some things we wish we had done differently. It's never too late to make a change and do things differently. Even if you had a child that you were not financially or mentally prepared for at the time, I'm sure you were able to figure out and be the best parent possible. My words of encouragement are "You never fail until you stop trying." Learn from past mistakes and embrace the lessons the experiences taught you and move forward to a brighter future.

Chapter XI.............. FUNDING CHILDREN'S COLLEGE EDUCATION

Are you familiar with a 529 Plan account? I'll admit, prior to becoming a parent, I was not all that familiar with a 529 plan. What I, absolutely, did know was that I wanted our daughter to be in a better financial position to attend college than we were. If you have children or are planning to have children in the near future, this is certainly a topic you want to be knowledgeable about. Let's take a further look.

A *529 Plan* is an education savings plan operated by the state or educational institution with many tax benefits, established to help families plan for future college expenses. It is named after section 529 of the Internal Revenue Code and was created in 1996. The legal name of a 529 Plan per the IRS is "Qualified Tuition Program." The savings plan can be used to attend any university, college or post-secondary training for your child or designated beneficiary. Each state has its own 529 plan and the structure may differ between states. It's important to look up your specific state's 529 plans. It is also a good idea to compare plans, as you are not limited to your particular state's plan.

Types of 529 Plans

There are two types of plans. One is a college savings plan and the other is a prepaid tuition plan. A *529 Prepaid Tuition Plan* allows you to pay for tuition ahead of time. The parent or legal guardian, as the purchaser, would have a contract with the state. You can pay for as many semesters as you'd like ahead of time and the contract ensures tuition, when the child is of age to attend college. Each state is allowed to offer both options. However, a qualified education institution can only offer the prepaid tuition option 529 plan. On the other hand, a *529 Savings Plan* allows the opportunity to earn higher returns by investing in stocks, bonds and mutual funds. You have the option to choose your portfolio allocation according to your level of risk aversion or comfort. Thus, the following information specifically pertains to the 529 savings plan option. This does not mean that some of these benefits aren't applicable to the prepaid plan as well.

There are many benefits associated with owning a 529 plan. The most significant benefit, as a parent or legal guardian, is the peace of mind you'll have knowing that you will be in a better position to afford your child's college education when the time comes. Here are some of the benefits and advantages:

✓ **Federal Tax Benefits**

There are many tax advantages for contributing to a 529 plan. Your investment grows tax-deferred. When the funds are withdrawn to cover tuition and other college related fees, distributions also come out federally tax-free. I will point out that the actual contributions made to the plan are not deductible on your federal tax returns.

✓ **State Tax Benefits**

In addition to federal tax benefits mentioned, depending upon what state you live in, your state may offer some tax breaks. For example, if you're a New York 529 plan account owner and have paid state taxes, you may be eligible to a maximum deduction of $5,000 if filed individually, or $10,000 if married and filing jointly. It's always a great idea to research your state's benefits.

✓ **Ease of Funding and Maintenance**

Most 529 plans has minimum balance requirement to open an account. Once the 529 plan is selected, a simple enrollment form is completed to select the contribution options to fund the account. You can opt to have direct deposit to make scheduled contributions. For example, if you choose to make monthly contributions to the plan, you can easily set up the account to draft the funds directly from your bank account. After that process is completed, there is nothing further for you to worry about. Hired finance professionals manage the assets in the account. You will not receive a Form 1099 to report taxes until the funds are withdrawn. Just wait until the funds are needed to put your little one (maybe not so little now) through college!

✓ **No Minimum Contribution Required**

For most 529 plans, there are no minimum contributions required for the account to remain open once you have met the initial requirement to open the account. You can choose the dollar amount you wish to contribute, and the frequency. For example, if you want to be aggressive and contribute $500 per month, that's great. On the other hand, if your budget only allow a contribution of $50 per month comfortably, that is still more savings than most likely you would have been saving. Perhaps, there's a month when you are unable to contribute to the account. No big deal, there are no penalties incurred for skipping a period. The point is, your savings adds up and grows over time.

If you elect to contribute a large yearly contribution at the beginning or end of the year, you may do so. However, there are contribution limits on the total yearly amount you can contribute to the account. Some plans allow you to contribute up to $300,000 per year in many states. I'm sure you're thinking, "That's a whole of money!" Yep, it is.

✓ **Gift Donations**

The plan allows gift donations as well. Instead of your child receiving tons of toys from family and friends during holidays and birthdays, the plan offers the opportunity for others to donate to the account as a gift. Most plans have printable gift certificates which are convenient and allow you to deliver to them during the special occasion. Of course, you may not be the favorite person in the room in their eyes, as they'd prefer the latest and greatest toy or electronic game, but they will appreciate you for it later. You will be investing into their lives and toward a brighter future!

✓ **Can I change beneficiary of a 529 Plan**

Yes. You can absolutely change the beneficiary of the 529 plan from one child to another without incurring any tax penalties. For example, perhaps you have an account for more than one child; you can roll over or transfer funds from one sibling's account to the other. Maybe the unthinkable happens (in your eyes) and your child decides college or post education just isn't for them. Maybe they have chosen to pursue other dreams immediately after graduating high school. After restraining yourself from tackling them, you still have the option of changing the designated beneficiary to another family member. Ultimately, they must have the dedication and commitment to pursue higher education as much as we, as parents, desire the best for them.

✓ **What if my child receives a full scholarship**

Of course, the reality is that every child will not have the academic ability or athleticism to land the opportunity of a full academic or athletic scholarship. If your son or daughter receives a full academic or athletic scholarship, your first thought is, "This is great news!" Your next thought is, "What happens to the funds that are no longer needed in the 529 account?" The good news is that there is no penalty incurred for withdrawing the funds in the event that your child, the beneficiary, receives a scholarship and the funds are no longer needed. In that case, you may simply withdraw the money or roll it over to another child, if that's a better alternative.

✓ **Rising Tuition Cost**

By investing in your child's future and education at an early age, ideally, before they even began formal schooling, you are setting them up for endless opportunities. As with other investments, the more time the assets are in the account, the more time they have to accrue earnings. Thus, the sooner the account is established for your son, daughter or grandchild, the better off you'll be to cover expenses for college. Most financial aid is given is in the form of student loans. While the interest on student loans is generally more favorable than other loans, it is still debt to be repaid nevertheless. Loan can take several years to repay. If you haven't set up a 529 plan, visit

www.savingforcolleg.com for additional information, or contact your

local bank and inquire about opening a 529 plan.

Chapter XII.............HOW TO TEACH FINANCIAL LESSONS TO CHILDREN

One of the greatest lessons you can share with your child is to teach financial responsibility. For some parents, the thought of discussing finances with your child creates an atmosphere of worry, panic or fear. You may think children shouldn't have to worry about such adult responsibilities. I strongly disagree with you, and I'll tell you why.

Children are naturally curious and inquisitive at an early age. The easiest way to teach this lesson is to simply incorporate it in your daily routines. They will emulate what they see from you, as parents. Start by establishing a budget or allowance. Be creative with it, try to make it fun! You can have them to pretend they are a banker, realtor, or financial advisor to introduce the value of a dollar. It's important to use elementary financial lessons and keep it interesting. Habits take root at a young age, good or bad, so it is essential that we plant the good seeds into our children.

As with many of life's great lessons we have an obligation to expose and teach them these invaluable lessons. In order to do so effectively, we have to practice what we are teaching to them. Too often, as parents, we expect our children to "do as we say, and not as we do." This motto is ineffective and received with resentment by children, especially teenagers. Here's what we can do. Start by having short conversations with you children and show them how mom and dad are making changes. If you don't pack lunch, incorporate packed lunch every day for a week and let them know how much money you've saved by making this change. Again, keep it light and fun. You can simply say, "Let's play a guessing game," and ask them how much money they think mom or dad saved by taking lunch. If they are a bit older, pre-teens or teens, you can follow the stock market performance with them. For example, have them pick one of their favorite social media companies such as Facebook or Twitter, or footwear companies such as Nike or Adidas and look at the movement of their stock performance. Encourage them to save their allowance money or earnings from summer jobs to own a few shares of their favorite companies.

Attempting to change everything all at once may be overwhelming. Begin with small incremental changes. It's easy to use similarities or comparison to our physical health when discussing financial health with kids. We'll assume potato chips, candy and soda are some favorites junk foods that kids like to snack on. Explain that after eating these foods often, we start to develop cavities and decay, which result in fillings and other dental problems. If we make wiser choices such as eating fruit, nuts, and drinking water instead of soda as a healthier alternative, we can avoid the dental problems. The same is true for our financial health. Buying costly items we may not need and overextending our credit will lead to financial destruction. Introduce allowances and budgets at an early age so your child will have an understanding and an appreciation for the value of a dollar. We've all heard the saying, "A penny saved is a penny earned." In simple terms, by saving at an early age, kids can reap huge payoffs in the long run with their parent's guidance.

You can also introduce your child to a minor's account, which you would open for him or her. A *minor's account* is a bank account set up by a parent to be used for a minor under the age of 18. The parent is responsible for this account prior to age 18, although the account is owned by the child. If your child receives an allowance or money on birthdays, let them allocate a percentage into their bank account.

Children are motivated, excited and encouraged by recognition. Positive reinforcement and visual acknowledgement are great. If you are computer savvy, you can plot their savings balance and create a chart for them to hang. This will serve as motivation for them to continue to save. Let them know that they are on the right track to smart decision making! One day, they may be the next investment banker or Warren Buffet, a financial genius. More importantly, they will be a wiser version of who they are meant to be!

Chapter XIII.................AVOID BEING HOUSE POOR

Have you ever heard of the term "house poor"? If you haven't, I'm sure you have a pretty good idea of what it could possibly mean, just from the words alone. The term "house poor" is used to describe the financial condition of a homeowner who spends the majority of their income on homeownership, and have difficulty meeting other financial obligations as a result.

Big Question: How does one become "House Poor?"

Unfortunately, what typically occurs is that the homeowner only considers the purchase price of the home. They fail to take into consideration the additional costs to maintain the home such as monthly utilities, property taxes, and periodic maintenance repairs. A common misconception most buyers have is the tendency to think that if the bank approves them for a specific loan amount, that's the purchase amount they can afford. This is not necessarily true. Lenders are in the business of making a profit and are only assessing whether you can meet the financial obligation to repay the loan. If you purchase a home at the very top of the approval amount, the majority of your income may be needed to cover the mortgage payment. You may find yourself in a situation where you have to forego making payment on other bills. This leads to the snowball effect. While you manage to keep a roof over your head, other bills began to pile up and outstanding debt gets bigger and bigger.

➤ Poor Financial Decision Making

What's shocking is that most people who are "house poor" usually earn a good income. The reason homeowners may find themselves in this situation is not because there isn't enough money coming in, instead, poor budgeting and mishandling of money is the culprit. If your spending habits exceed your incoming earnings, the reality is, you'll have a very difficult time paying all of your living expenses. For example, consider the middle class homeowner who has a college degree, earns well above the average U.S. household income and is still house poor. They may have landed the perfect job and jumped right into buying the latest and greatest electronics, car and home. Despite earning a great salary, their check is consumed by the mortgage and there is little money left. Instead of buying a home immediately, a better financial choice would have been to rent a modest apartment and accumulate a nest egg before moving into a home.

➤ Loss of Income

If there is an unexpectedly loss of income in the household and there isn't adequate savings, this could also lead to becoming house poor. Many people have faced misfortune in the past recent years during massive layoffs. As a result of loss of income, you may go from living comfortably and having discretionary income to take great family vacations, to having just enough income to just cover living expenses.

➢ Living Beyond Your Financial Means

The perception most people have as it relates to living beyond one's means is probably someone who only buys designer shoes and clothing, drives an expensive car and lives an extravagant lifestyle. Not true at all. That's the misconception. There are many people who love to go shopping and splurge on expensive items, but are able to afford that lifestyle and cover their living expenses, and are in good financial health.

On the other hand, take the homeowner who makes six figures, or more. You may wonder how they can become house poor. It's the exact same way someone that earns an average income becomes house poor. The difference is that there's a much larger scale to spend money. The higher the income, the more expensive the home tends to be, therefore, you have higher living expenses. Again, if the income earned cannot support the lifestyle, you'll find that you can barely meet mortgage payments. Even worst, living beyond what you can comfortably afford can ultimately result in foreclosure. Sadly, I've seen numerous million dollar homes that were foreclosed because homeowners purchased homes and were unable to continuously meet the financial obligations.

What Can You Do to Avoid Becoming House Poor?

➢ Purchase a Home You Can Afford on One Income

The best advice I can give to avoid becoming house poor, hands down, is to establish a budget for a home that can be met using one household income. As stated earlier, relying on one income will allow you to have discretionary income to allocate elsewhere. If you're a single homeowner, avoid using the maximum approval amount when house hunting. For example, let's assume you're approved for $350,000 by the bank. Do not allow your maximum approval amount to be the budget for your home, instead, set your budget between 80%-85% of that amount. This way, you've given yourself a buffer. Essentially, you've created a shield to protect yourself from purchasing a home that consumes the majority of your income.

> **Stick to your budget**

Many people may set a budget when searching for their perfect home. That's easy. The hard part is being disciplined enough to stand firm and adhere to the budget you've set. Don't overextend yourself financially. It's very easy to be persuaded by a realtor who may suggest that the property isn't much higher than your max budget, or by a spouse who falls in love with the house at first sight and persuades you that it's still affordable. You want to be realistic in what you can and cannot afford, and want to certainly avoid relying on two or three jobs just to pay your mortgage. By sticking to what you can afford up front, you'll avoid the stress and will be glad you did.

> **Ask for Estimate Property Tax, HOA Fees and Utilities**

Property taxes, homeowner's association fees and monthly utilities will account for a substantial portion of overall costs of homeownership. Many people fail to take these additional expenses into consideration during their house hunt. Remember, these costs will be in addition to the mortgage payments, which are assessed on the purchase price of the home.

What I've learned, after becoming a homeowner, is that estimated expenses are available by the selling agent for the property you're considering buying, particularly if it was previously occupied. Having a good estimate of these costs up front will help you determine if the total monthly living expenses will consume your entire salary. If so, you want to avoid purchasing this home and continue your search. Although this may mean you'll have to forego immediate gratifications, you'll be much happier and less financially burdened in the long-term.

> ### Set aside savings for unexpected repairs

Long gone are the days when you can call your landlord or property manager to replace the water heater or light fixtures. As a homeowner, you have the sole financial responsibility for the up-keep of your home and property. While I don't want to alarm you, I do want to create an awareness of the inevitable repairs and maintenance expenses that will undoubtedly arise with homeownership. Once you consider potential costs up front and have an adequate savings, shall they occur; you can avoid being house poor and live comfortably.

According to Freddie Mac, homeowners will spend between 1 to 4 percent of a home's value annually on maintenance and repairs, which usually increases as the house ages. At first glance, these numbers may not seem insignificant, but when you do the math, the dollar amount can be pretty hefty. For example, on a home that is valued at $250,000, you can spend as much as $10,000 on the higher end, which is the equivalent of 4 percent. On the lower end of the spectrum at 1 percent, this still leaves the average homeowner with $2,500 in annual expenses. Be mindful that if you purchase a new construction home or a recently remodeled home, you may not incur repairs in the first few years. If you're considering buying an older home, having a home inspection before purchasing the home is the best way to discover any potential issues with the structure of the home. After the inspection, you can make an informed decision of whether to proceed or pass up on buying the house.

Owning a homeowner's insurance policy is another great investment to protect your home and family. Having a broad coverage policy can cover damages from unfortunate events such as fires, floods and other catastrophic events. Without a policy in place, such occurrences can leave you financially burdened and unable to occupy a safe home for your family. By being proactive, we can prepare ourselves financially for many unexpected events and limit the hardship that can happen all at once. Many of you may have heard of the infamous saying, "When it rains, it pours." Well, I'm sure you'd all agree it's so much better when you have your umbrella of protection! That's what a home insurance policy gives, that added protection.

Chapter XIV.................HOW TO REBUILD CREDIT WORTHINESS

As a result of insufficient repayment and over spending, the consequence suffered is unsatisfactory credit history. Consequently, it's difficult or impossible to obtain a line of credit with major lenders. If you manage to secure a credit line, you'll incur unfavorable, extremely high, borrowing rates. Regardless of how we managed to get into this situation, our credit history follows us. The good news is that it is not too late to rebuild your credit.

The key to rebuilding your credit history is sheer determination, willingness and persistent to get out of debt and curtail your spending habits. It's completely up to you! That's first and foremost. It will certainly be a long road and will not happen overnight. Nothing in life is easy, especially rebuilding credit history. It's actually easier to destroy credit than to rebuild it.

You absolutely must be willing to make financial sacrifices and be willing to cut back on unnecessary expenditures. The best way to begin the process of rebuilding your credit is to review your credit card statements as well as obtain a free copy of your credit score. You can simply go to *www.annualcreditreport.com* and request your free credit report from Equifax, Transunion and Experian. This site is secure and is authorized by the Federal law.

The report will show both good standing and default accounts from the beginning of your credit history. You should begin reviewing the report to identify any outstanding accounts which are in default. Once identified, the objective is to resolve these accounts. Begin by contacting the vendors to inquire about repayment options.

If you've had the courage to confront your financial health, you have just taken a huge leap! When you think of your physical health, often times, many of us are afraid to go to the doctors to address the underlying issue of what's causing the pain. We try to ignore the ailment and pain associated with it in hopes that the issue will resolve itself. The reality is that severe illnesses do not just go away on its own without seeking medical intervention. In comparison to our financial health, the same is true. When there are severe problems such as insufficient credit scores, defaults on loans, etc., we need to face the issue head on. Seek the professional help of a financial advisor to assist in resolving these problems if they are too overwhelming for you to handle.

Now that you've been able to obtain your credit history report, the real work begins. Be prepared to make some sacrifices off the bat. You have to rebuild trust with lenders and prove that you can make payments on time and consistently. I've put together a list of tips to help you on this journey:

> **Change Your Spending Habits**

I'm sure you've all heard the familiar saying, "You cannot do the same things and expect different results." The same is true here. You have to alter your spending habits to begin to rebuild your credit worthiness, that's a must.

➤ Establish New Credit

If you no longer hold a major credit card and have not been able to secure one, begin by applying for one at your local department store, home improvement store such as Home Depot or Lowes, or a gas station. The objective is to slowly rebuild your credit history to prove to major financial institutions that you can be trusted with borrowed capital, and will repay in a timely manner. You only want to apply to one or two, at the most. Too many inquiries on your credit will make you appear less attractive to lenders.

➤ Repay Immediately

Not only will repaying your credit card balance immediately help to rebuild your credit, it will also prevent you from going down this road again. Creditors are actually anticipating that most credit card holders will not make early repayment, thus, gaining additional earnings on interest fees charged. Remember, the goal in using a minor credit card is to rebuild our credit history. Only use the card if you have available cash to pay it off immediately. Never carry over your balance to the next billing cycle. One simple rule to remember, "If you don't have the money for it, you can't afford it." This will help to keep you on track to your quest to restoring creditworthiness.

➤ Never Max Out Your Credit Card

It's never a good idea to use the total available credit line. The likelihood that you can repay the full amount on a maxed-out credit card is very slim to unlikely, particularly, when you have a past credit history that does not reflect good standings and high credit risk. It's a good rule of thumb to avoid this situation. Financial experts recommended that you stay below 30% of your available credit limit. In a nutshell, using the maximum credit allowed creates the illusion of financial security that you do not possess. When rebuilding your credit trustworthiness, you do not want to continue past negative habits. Maxing credit cards is one of the culprits which leads to unfavorable credit standings.

> **Continue to Monitor Your Credit Report**

Request a copy of your credit report once every four months from one of the major credit bureaus (Equifax, Experian, Transunion). Be proactive and consistent. Ensure you review the report for any discrepancies and be prepared to follow up and dispute any activity that is inaccurate.

If you stick to these habits, over time, you will begin to improve your credit history. Not only will you repair and rebuild your credit scores, you will find you have gained control of your spending habits and self-discipline as well. In the long run, you'll be in better financial position while achieving the ultimate goal of rebuilding satisfactory credit history.

I deeply and sincerely encourage you to take the next step and implement these lessons. Have the conversation with others to encourage someone else. Walk into a brighter financial future of empowerment and freedom.